The Secular Ten-Step Program Workbook

By Robert Villegas

The Secular Ten-Step Program Workbook

By

Robert Villegas

Contact: rville9755@aol.com

ISBN 1539397785

Published in the United States of America.

Series Title: Villegas Self-Improvement Volume 1

Dedicated to My Father

Robert Regino

Table of Contents

"Is it the gods...who put in our hearts / This burning desire...or else / Does each man make of his own wild yearning a god?"

-

Virgil, The Aeneid

This book is based upon my book *Alcoholism and Addiction – A Secular Ten-Step Program* which spells out an alternative to the AA 12-Step Program. It is intended to function as a workbook which will help you work through the issues of addiction and relate them to your own thought processes and values. It is published in small format so it can fit in your pocket or briefcase readily available for you to jot down your ideas and thoughts through your daily activities.

I am going to provide a clear workbook here that focuses on the ten steps of the process discussed in the wider book. I would suggest you read this book before you start working through the ten steps. It will provide you with a wider perspective and give you a better foundation for understanding addiction.

This workbook can also be handed out to patients by counsellors and psychologists in order to provide material for counselling sessions and even group discussions for people who are required to attend counselling and group sessions as part of their sentence handed down by a judge. I would suggest that counsellors desiring to use the Secular Ten-Step Program keep several copies of both the book, this handbook as well as the other handbook that will be based on the group counselling aid "The World's First Drunk".

THE TEN-STEP PROGRAM

STEP 1. LIBERATE YOURSELF

In order to properly direct your life, you must become an independent thinker. I'm not talking about reading every major philosopher, two newspapers a day and five books a week. I'm merely talking about doing the best you can to think with your own mind rather than follow what you are told by so-called authority figures, peers, parents and other family members. Certainly, we love them but you have a responsibility to yourself to get your life right and you have to start with what happens inside your own head.

The key to starting this liberation is to do an assessment of how independent you are regarding decisions you make for your life. Here are a few questions to ask:

1. Do you often change your mind or feel uncomfortable when someone disagrees with you or criticizes something you do?

_____

_____

_____

_____

_____

_____

_____
_____
_____
_____
_____
_____
_____

2. Is your first thought about any issue what other people think rather than what you think?

_____
_____
_____
_____
_____
_____
_____
_____
_____
_____
_____

3. Do you prefer to investigate an issue and study it to define what you think or do you just ask others?

_____
_____
_____
_____
_____
_____
_____
_____

_____

_____

_____

_____

Thinking for yourself is not an easy habit to get into. It requires some basic knowledge of how good thinking is done and even a little bit of courage.

I think that thinking for yourself is essential to defeating addiction. And you will find that it is enjoyable and beneficial to learn to be independent. There are plenty of good books that will teach you how to think clearly and I'd suggest that you buy one or two. You will be glad you did. Place the name of each book here and mention some of the ideas you learned from them:

_____

_____

_____

_____

_____

_____

_____

_____

_____

_____

_____

The best advice I can give you in the short amount of space we have is to develop the habit of looking at reality first when you have a question. Avoid looking for the opinions of others (unless they are experts in their field) and don't hesitate to ask probing questions and develop your own conclusions.

One thing you should do, at this point, is to read the chapter on theory in the Appendix to my book (*Alcoholism and Addiction – A Secular Ten-Step Program*). Try to understand, as best as you can, that addiction is an approach to pain. As an individual, you have encountered physical and psychological pain and you selected a particular out-of-context approach based upon an emphasis on pleasure in order to deal with the pain. Below, write some of your thoughts as you read through this chapter:

_____

_____

_____

_____

_____

_____

_____

_____

_____

_____

_____

_____

I would suggest that you use this journal to help you answer these questions:

- How have I habitually used pleasure to deal with my pain?

_____

_____

_____
_____
_____
_____
_____
_____
_____
_____
_____
_____

- What has given me pain?

_____
_____
_____
_____
_____
_____
_____
_____
_____
_____

- What is my physical pain?

_____
_____
_____
_____
_____

_____

_____

_____

_____

_____

_____

- What is my mental pain?

_____

_____

_____

_____

_____

_____

_____

_____

_____

_____

- What caused these?

_____

_____

_____

_____

_____

_____

_____

_____

_____

- How can I change the thinking that requires that I try to escape my pain?

_____

_____

_____

_____

_____

_____

_____

_____

_____

- What can I do to confront my pain and relieve it without addiction?

_____

_____

_____

_____

_____

_____

_____

_____

_____

_____

- What must I change in my own mind in order to understand this process of dealing with pain through acceptance of my addiction?

_____
_____
_____
_____
_____
_____
_____
_____
_____
_____
_____
_____

Keep this journal with you at all times and while you are sitting alone, waiting at the car dealership, sitting in your car on a bench in the park. Spend lots of time on these questions and see where they lead you. Try to convert your discoveries into actions? As you go through these steps, the answers to your questions will help you have a broader perspective on your problems and help you with the other parts of the ten-step program.

Place your action plan there:

_____
_____
_____
_____
_____
_____

_____

_____

_____

_____

_____

_____

_____

_____

_____

_____

_____

_____

_____

_____

_____

_____

_____

STEP 2. MAKE A LIST OF YOUR VALUES.

I am not going to tell you how to live your life. I will only say this: you have a problem and that problem is derived from how you think. There are good influences in society and there are bad but the responsibility to "get it right" is yours and yours alone. You have to straighten out the mess. I have tried to give you some guidelines and ideas on the way forward. I hope you find them helpful.

The most important thing you can do is regain your control of your life and this requires accepting your personal responsibility for doing that. You need to know how to think about you and what you need to do to correct your past mistakes.

You are responsible for yourself. If you make a mistake in thinking, you will also make a mistake in acting. You need to understand how you make your mistakes and, more importantly, you need to understand how to avoid making those mistakes in the future.

How can you do this? It is all about values; the right values; values that clearly benefit your life.

You will find this an interesting exercise that will give you new insights into your life. Remember the definition of values as having the standard of life. Now we will engage in a process that helps you define your values, organize them and appreciate their importance for you.

For this step, write down the things you value most in whatever order they come to you. Don't forget values such as your children, loved ones, and your goals such as a college degree or getting a raise, anything that you pursue in order to advance your life, knowledge, happiness, condition of living, etc.

Now, before we work on these values, I'd like to suggest that you put at the top a special category of values called "Cardinal Values". I would recommend "reason, purpose and self-esteem[1] as three Cardinal Values that will help you make all the others possible.

---

[1] These are the three cardinal values that Ayn Rand included in her discussion of the topic of values in her book The Virtue of Selfishness. http://amzn.to/2aOPB3q

If you are going to understand why you want to engage in harmful activities, you need to use your best thinking. In some cases, you are going to have to make an effort to learn how to think so you are no longer lying to yourself. You'll even need to use your mind to understand how to accomplish your values and how to keep from self-destructive behavior. This is reason.

Additionally, you need a clearly defined purpose in life if you are going to put yourself on a path toward success. It may take some effort to define your purpose but you'll find that the effort is well worth it because your purpose can be a beacon that will help you know when you are straying from your overall goal of achieving your ultimate values. Ask yourself what is the over-arching thing that you would like to dedicate your life to accomplishing. What defines you and your life in terms of your ultimate goals? Then distill the answers to a singular purpose (you can also have sub-purposes as well but it is important to limit your main purpose to one fundamental accomplishment).

Finally, you need a sense of self. You have to want to respect and appreciate yourself more than you do at the present time. The likelihood is that your self-esteem is often taking some hits as you continue to engage in your harmful behavior so you need to start building yourself up to help give you a reason to do the right thing for yourself.

With that said, the first thing you should do is to stop thinking in terms of failure or success. Going off the wagon, so to speak, at least when you are getting started on your quest to regain your life, is not the end of the world. You should learn to treat any "failure" you experience as a chance to learn what is going on in your mind.

When you do go off the wagon, don't excoriate yourself and insult yourself. Examine what was going on in your mind at the time and write it down. Then use it as a reference point the next time you are tempted. Learn to use these "failures" as opportunities to learn about your inner mind so you can understand yourself better. Stop beating yourself up. This is a process not a commandment.

The Cardinal values I suggested above will provide a structure to your value system so you need to think through why you need them and how they will work together to help you plan and organize your life around positive living. Please take whatever time you need to convince yourself. If you have any questions, please check with your counsellor.

Hopefully, I've convinced you that these cardinal values should go at the top of your list. To help make them concrete in your mind, you should also add these values: rationality, productiveness, pride like this:

Reason	Purpose	Self-esteem
Rationality	Productiveness	Pride

These additional three values are directly related to the Cardinal values. Rationality is your commitment to think rationally and act rationally. Productiveness is how you will achieve your purpose. You will work, create values to trade with others, develop your work skills, etc. and Pride is the expression of your respect for yourself and how you will conduct yourself in all phases of your life. Now we can turn to your list.

The first thing you want to do with your list is arrange it in the order of importance. Put the most important values at the top of the list and arrange them toward the bottom with the least important value last. Throughout this process, you'll want to add or remove values as you see fit. Again, this is not a legal document so just put things down as you think about them. Later, as you see a need, you can adjust these values or even add additional values.

Here's the list I came up with for you:

Self
- Playing tennis
- Keeping myself fit
- A nice pair of shoes

Family
- My wife
- My children
- New tires for my car
- Helping my mother

Home
- A good home
- A 4K Big Screen TV

Career
- A promotion at work

- A new suit
- A new computer

You'll notice that I've created categories for values that relate to specific contexts. I call these "buckets" but you can call them categories if you'd like. This approach also enables you to concentrate on one category during the context in which you are situated in that context. For instance, you have to work Monday through Friday so you can concentrate on your value hierarchy for "career" during those times. Now that you know which values are most important within that category, you can schedule certain times to focus on creating "to-do lists" that focus on those values. Each sub-value or "step", once it is completed can be scratched off the list so you can move to the next step.

Your "Personal" category may have many more values in it because it represents your own special context for developing yourself, your interests and likes. This is most likely an enjoyable part of your value structure but notice that I've put it at the top and hold it to be the most important category. Of course, this is optional. It really depends on one thing: reality. But, in my view, the reality is that only you can be that important to yourself that you'd want to put yourself first.

That's right, reality. Every one of your values should be tied to reality and related to the standard of what is good for your life. Why is this important? You have to have a clear certainty about your values. You have to know that they are real or can be made real through your productive ability. In fact, a big part of your confusion about your actions and behaviors is related to uncertainty about your values.

If this confuses you, it may be because you have been taught to distrust reality. Yet, Aristotle taught us long ago the essential truth that can help us understand reality. In essence, he said that A is A (the law of identity) and this means that every entity in the world is a distinct entity that can be understood by identifying its characteristics. Add the law of identity to the law of cause and effect and you have the principle that things act according to their distinguishing characteristics in a given context.

Why is this important? What do philosophical issues have to do with your bad habits?

Good questions. The answer is that your approach to life has a starting point. This means that your understanding of the nature of reality and how to think in the real world are part of your psychological foundation, the two subjects you think about most often without even knowing about it (what is real and how do I know it?). In other words, you are always consumed by two questions in life.

What does this have to do with your bad behavior? What does this have to do with your self-destruction? Everything. Here's why: Before you can decide to pick up that drink, you must have a reason for it. You must know that doing so will accomplish something for you (either good or bad). So you must have an understanding of the nature of reality. It is knowledge of reality that gives you the information that picking up the drink will make you feel better. So the question of what you know and how you know it is critical.

If your core conscious values are positive and defensible; which means you have connected them to reality and they have a clear benefit for you, you can then easily identify those harmful subconscious core values and eliminate them.

So, let's take the next step. Go through your list and find out where your particular addiction is located. Let's make sure it gets on the list because you know, at this point, it is an important value for you and it must be integrated into your core values.

Let's say we come up with this list:

Self
- Playing tennis
- Going to the bar
- Keeping myself fit
- A nice pair of shoes

Family
- My wife
- My children
- A relaxing drink at home
- New tires for my car
- Helping my mother

Home
- A good home
- A 4K Big Screen TV

- A bar

Career
- Enjoying drinks with my fellow workers
- A promotion at work
- A new suit
- A new computer

Regarding your values in the category of "yourself", doesn't "going to the bar" seem out of place? The only way it could not be out of place is if it were not a value. Sitting at a bar for hours and getting drunk takes you away from developing yourself. What is the proper conclusion to draw from this?

How about that relaxing drink at home in your "Family" category? That may not be too bad but it could also be a rationalization that drinking is merely an innocent family activity. Nothing wrong with dad having a drink while the family sits on the couch to watch a movie.

There are several problems with this, not the least of which is what it communicates to your children. This can be especially confusing when they see Dad acting "uncharacteristically" and frequently getting playful, for instance wrestling with the kids and being overly generous when they ask him for a new toy or to go to the local amusement center whereupon Dad may need to drive drunk. Or it could mean your wife getting upset with you because you have blown the family budget in taking the family out.

All of this tells the kids Dad acts differently when he is drinking and sometimes Mom has to carry him to bed because he might fall over. How do all these "benign" family activities disrupt the family and work against your values for your family? Are you going to rationalize them and pretend they don't matter? Perhaps your wife does not rationalize them and thinks less of you as a man.

Now let's look at that bar you'd like to add to your home. Certainly, it implies that you think drinking is something that should be done often in a home. Of course the homes of rich people frequently are populated with classy bars and shiny glasses and a fully stocked cabinet. But do you really wish to spend hours of the day drinking? Do you really plan to have lots of parties with your neighbors and associates?

What about enjoying a drink with your fellow workers? Of course, you work hard and it is great to wind down the weekend and spend some time relaxing. Yet, have you noticed that some of your fellow workers always say "No" when asked if they'd like to join? Or have you noticed that after one drink other fellow workers go home? And over time, even these fellow workers decide not to participate. Have you noticed that now only a couple of you are left at the bar and that you are both drunk? At some point, your boss notices that you are hungover during the week and he begins to question your production and wonders what is happening with your personal life. Perhaps that harmless drink after work is not so harmless.

After thinking this through, perhaps it is better to remove those "drinking values" from your list and your life. This is not as easy as it seems but you've taken a big step in realizing the truth about drinking and living. You might consider replacing them with some more healthful and positive values.

The process of establishing your values will take time. You should spend lots of time thinking about each of these values, how you will accomplish them, what sub-values they imply and how you will accomplish these as well. This process will help you get your mind straight and help you learn to avoid thinking about non-values and addictions that contradict your values. This means you should be thinking about this list virtually all the time, get it inside of you, and make it your constant thought.

STEP 3. FEEL YOUR VALUES

But this is more than just a list. You should learn to experience your values because of their importance in your life. Learn to feel them and how much they mean to you, especially those values that are fundamental to your life, your mind, your needs and especially those people you love. They are not just lines on a piece of paper, they are the reason you live. It can help you tremendously to learn just how deeply you love them and how much they mean to you especially when you compare them to the artificial and poorly chosen disvalues that are harming your life. See your true values in perspective and put your disvalues in their proper place as unimportant things you really don't value at all.

Now go through each value you have written down above and ask yourself how strongly you feel about this value. How much does it mean to you? Be as expressive and deep as possible and especially compare it to how much you want your addiction. Which has a more powerful attraction to you and why?

_____
_____
_____
_____
_____
_____
_____
_____
_____
_____
_____
_____
_____
_____
_____
_____
_____
_____
_____
_____
_____
_____
_____
_____
_____
_____

_____

_____

_____

_____

_____

_____

_____

_____

The critical point for you always comes at the time when your feelings and your reason conflict. Your troublesome emotions are based upon your past faulty thinking; they give you your rationalizations and they drive your body to do what you subconsciously want to do. It feels like your body "needs" the addiction and you have convinced yourself that fighting the "needs" of your body is unhealthful. This is the decision point where you need to confront your bad emotions, question them and defeat them for their irrationality. This will help you create a new decision point that is based upon your self-interest and values.

It is at this point where you need to convince yourself that your emotions are wrong; that they are based upon false premises and at that point of decision, you must say "No" to your desire for the addiction. It is at this point, when you are literally flying blind, driven to the satisfaction of the addiction that you can stop yourself – but you must keep in your mind the fact that now, under the power of the false emotion, you cannot stop yourself. You must engage yourself at every turn when the false emotion is driving you so that the debate within becomes conscious and open; and once you arrive at full consciousness of the irrational decision, you will begin to develop, by means of the principle of opposites, to begin the process of changing your action, basing it on reason, positive, correct facts (knowledge) and this will change your emotion that drives you toward a more positive value and life-serving decision.

The better you get this thought process out into the open, the better for you. The more you engage in the process, the closer you will get to understanding what is going on inside your mind and the better you will be at controlling it and making the right decisions.

Some tips:

1. If you fail, it isn't the end of the world. It merely means that you are programmed too strongly toward your addictive behavior. You just have to try to do better next time. Mentally record what you thought in that moment of decision and especially make sure your record how strongly your subconscious fought to make you do it. This will serve you well when that moment of decision comes again. You will know what to expect. The more times you make these mental notes, the stronger will be your ability to prepare for what to expect next time so you get everything clear in your mind.

2. You need independence of thought. It is easy to fall back into thinking the way other people think. We've been taught to do that all our lives. But it is critical on this point that you think independently and avoid, as much as possible, following old ways

of thinking. It is your life; not the life of other people. It is your mind and you must pave your own path if you are going to understand yourself.

The key point is that moment of decision. It is there where the inner-deception takes place. It at this moment where you can catch yourself. Ask yourself to be more specific about your reason for choosing the activity. For instance, "Why do you think you need to eat right now?" "Who are you trying to please in consenting to this activity?" Be as precise as you can and try to dig deep into what is going on in your mind. Make it explicit so you can check the facts and argue against it.

STEP 4. STOP LYING TO YOURSELF AND START TRUTHING

The basic premise of this step is to realize that, deep down inside, you want your addiction or choice of pleasure. You have given your mind a command to lie to you and you have deliberately agreed to accept that lie by deciding to engage in destructive behavior. This now subconscious desire (emotion) enables actions that are contrary to your chosen values.

As we saw in step two, by defining your values and listing them as we have suggested, you are able to identify contradictions in your values. You also obtain the ability to think about them in explicit terms and this is a big step toward resolving the value contradiction. Now you have to identify the lies that you have told your mind to tell you.

"Once you have validated your moral code, if properly

done, you have only the choice to be moral or immoral. If your morality is "for you", your highest amoral maxim is to live life to the fullest. Once you accomplish this, you have no choice but to follow that morality to the extreme. You can't simply say that you'll be moral part of the time or that you'll only be half-moral. You are either moral or you are immoral. And, it is a choice of life or death."[2]

Needless to say, you should look carefully over your value list and try to write down as clearly as possible the contradictions in your values and identify how these contradictions affect your choices. Each contradiction is an indication that your values are at cross-purposes.

Let's examine the contradictions in the list of values we have created. Write your list down again and with each category insert your addictive "values". You can add actions like "Going to the bar" or "Relaxing at home with a drink", making a bar in the family room" and other such values. Put them in their correct "bucket" and then we'll analyze them.

_____
_____
_____
_____
_____
_____
_____
_____
_____
_____
_____
_____

---

[2] The Age of Selfishness by Robert Villegas, kindle version, Anti-man

_____

_____

_____

_____

_____

_____

_____

_____

_____

_____

_____

_____

_____

_____

_____

_____

_____

_____

_____

_____

_____

_____

_____

_____

_____

_____

_____

_____

Look at each one of these addictive values and ask yourself:

Doesn't it conflict with other values? In what way does it

conflict?

_____

_____

_____

_____

_____

_____

_____

_____

Doesn't it make achieving your other values more difficult? In what way?

_____

_____

_____

_____

_____

_____

_____

You could be playing tennis with that time and you could buy a new pair of shoes with the money that you spent on your addiction. But there is always the chance that if you leave the bar drunk and try to drive, you will be arrested by a cop and have to undergo jail, a trial, group therapy, psycho-analysis, possibly even divorce and losing your kids.

How could you advance your values for yourself with all of these distractions?

_____

_____

_____

_____

_____

_____

_____

Let's stay on this for a while. I want to go deeper into the arguments (facts) that your mind would seek to find in order to place "going to the bar" into your hierarchy of values. It is with the decision to go to engage in the addiction that you are giving your mind the order to find those facts and present them to you as valid reasons why it is *not* a contradiction of your values.

This is the thought process that you need to isolate and observe so you can get an objective view of what is happening inside your mind. Here is an over view:

1. You found early in life a specific pleasure that helped you evade the requirements of living and/or thinking – it helped you with your fears.
2. You chose this pleasure as a value merely because it made you feel better.
3. You learned that the value was largely considered to be destructive.
4. You told your mind to find "facts" or arguments that enabled you to engage in the pleasurable activity.
5. These arguments became part of your moral code and conflicted with your other positive values.
6. Look at your values and see how some of them contradict each other.
7. Stop telling your mind to lie to you. This is the critical point where you must argue with yourself in

order to arrive at a point where the arguments "for" the value are challenged.

8. Argue with yourself every time you find yourself telling your mind to justify these contradictory actions.
9. Develop the habit of truthing and never letting your mind lie to you.
10. As with most things that require skills, repetition of these arguments is critical to your success. Careful note taking of your thoughts can be very helpful.

Of all of the above, which apply to you? How did you let this happen?

_____

_____

_____

_____

_____

_____

_____

_____

_____

_____

_____

_____

_____

"Needless to say, there are a great many investigations that an individual will need to make in order to arrive at a point of developing his or her moral code. Metaphysical issues regarding the nature of reality, the ability of man's mind to ascertain reality, the nature of concepts and the reasoning process are issues that each individual should pursue before he can begin to choose the purpose and values he will pursue."[3]

This is why we are here trying to put order to your values. You need your mind to identify your values and how to pursue and acquire them. You need to have a clear picture of what you are working for and why.

So now, let's look at what you left behind in your past. You may not realize this (and this is part of the problem) but there are values which you have probably left off your list. These are values that you developed very early in life that are now subconscious. These values may contradict your chosen values because they were chosen when you were so young that you don't remember them.

Look at what you are doing now to contradict your values list and ask yourself what happened in your past that got you to a point of wanting something that might not have been good for you. Write your answers down here:

_____
_____
_____
_____
_____
_____
_____
_____
_____

---

[3] The Age of Selfishness by Robert Villegas, kindle version, The Benefits of Being Selfish

_____

_____

_____

_____

_____

Now that you've gone through a thorough analysis of your values and found the contradictions, you must "automatize" the thought process that will remove the contradictions and create a moral code based in integrity. But this isn't so easy. You still have those earlier arguments that have gone "underground" in your subconscious. Those arguments keep telling you that your contradictions are justified. Look at the list above about how people think about their addictions and how they communicate to their own minds; this is a sort of infinite loop intended to find "facts" and arguments to engage in the harmful pleasures. You need to understand this process thoroughly and use it to monitor your thought process as you seek to change and improve your moral life. Let's identify the specific situations you find yourself in (or put yourself into) where you start arguing for your addiction. How can you avoid putting yourself into that situation? What can you do to stay away from it?

_____

_____

_____

_____

_____

_____

_____

_____

_____

_____

_____

_____

_____

_____

_____

_____

_____

Have this list with you at all times; use these pages to help you walk through your thought process so you can monitor it at times when you have a moment and would like to keep the process clear in your mind. It will help you gain your moral footing and keep you on track.

You should keep in mind that whenever you do something solely for pleasure, you are more than likely contradicting your other values in some way. For instance, eating for pleasure becomes such a habit that you are constantly eating in violation of your value of being healthy. When you rationalize eating for pleasure because "you deserve it", you are lying to yourself so you can do something that you want to do. That pleasure is more important than your own life and that threatens your life.

This last point is critical because you need to start identifying those things that threaten your life and avoid them like the plague. They must become so odious and distasteful for you that you never want to do them again. Yet, this process only requires that you learn what they are and how harmful they are to your values and life.

A good way of getting the right perspective on your addictive behavior is to realize that you are telling your mind to lie to you about the idea that your addictive behavior is good for you. This is a reversal of correct thinking. If something is, in fact, bad for you, you should not want it. So if you find that you do want it, you must identify the arguments you make that are "working" to keep you doing them and evaluate those arguments for what they are: harmful and even deadly.

Another way of understanding this position (that will help you understand yourself) is to ask yourself a hypothetical question. If your life is going better than you had ever hoped. If everything is happening in your life perfectly and beyond your hopes and dreams and you are incredibly happy with everything and everyone in your life, would you even think about engaging in your addiction of choice? If you knew that your addiction would cause all of your greatest dreams to tumble down like a house of cards, would you even be tempted to engage in it?

The questions can help you clarify just how dangerous your addiction of choice really is and it should serve as a solid reason why you should stay away from it with certainty and conviction.

You should learn to argue with yourself. For instance, late one night when you decide you want a muffin and a cup of hot cocoa, you should realize that you don't need them and are putting additional calories, sugars, cholesterol and other chemicals into your body and harming your health. By arguing with yourself, you can find reasons why eating now is harming. You may not always win this argument but it is important to keep arguing until you start winning.

At this point, write down your best arguments for not engaging in your addictive behavior. How do they threaten the values you love?

_____
_____
_____
_____
_____
_____
_____
_____
_____
_____
_____
_____
_____
_____
_____
_____
_____
_____
_____

As I mentioned before, at this early stage, it is not necessary to prevent yourself from having these urges. They are the result of your body's craving the addiction. The important thing is not to "guilt" yourself. What will eventually stop you is when you have completely "undone" your rationalizations through reason. At that point, the urges will dissipate. It won't be easy but it may not be as hard as you think as long as you keep using your mind.

Here is some room for more notes:

_____

_____

_____

STEP 5. THE PRINCIPLE OF OPPOSITES

Another way to deal with these subconscious arguments about your pleasure choices is to use the principle of opposites. Simply put it means taking a bad thought and thinking in reverse, in its opposite.

This method can be particularly effective when you are trying to rationalize positive arguments for harmful behavior. It involves:

1. Knowing that your arguments for violating your values are wrong.
2. Knowing that they are subconscious and difficult to excise.
3. Saying the opposite of the false argument and emphasizing it emotionally by thinking of the negative consequences of defending the action.
4. Repeating the argument as many times as possible.
5. Developing a distaste for the addiction.

Make a list of your negative values and the arguments you make for each of them. Then write down the opposite argument.

_____

_____

_____

_____

_____

_____

_____

_____

Once you have identified a good argument against the addiction (using this method), read it over when you are alone or waiting at the dealership for your car to be repaired or standing in line somewhere. The key here is repetition and improvement of the argument.

Let's look at an example:

When my mind lies to me that it is perfectly normal to go to the bar at any time, those arguments can be met by the opposite argument: going to the bar is irrational, it is not normal, it is dangerous if I drink too much and get arrested, my children don't like seeing me come home drunk. These arguments are actually better than lying to yourself. They are the anti-thesis of the lies you tell yourself, and in this case, they are the truth. Write them all down in your diary.

Telling yourself the opposite of your rationalization is one way that you can discover that you are lying to yourself. Get into the habit of doing this and you'll find that, over time, you'll have less incentive to go to the bar and more incentive to do positive things like teach your boys/girls how to play ball and give them the attention they need and deserve.

An equally effective attitude is to draw the worst possible picture you can of the consequences of "going to the bar". See yourself as knockout drunk, teetering while you walk, bumping into a door, having an accident. Exaggeration here is not even a lie – it may, in fact, actually happen (or has already happened). Do you really want to live like this? Keep asking yourself that question.

The principle of opposites can provide a glimpse into just how much your mind is lying to you and just how much you want it to lie to you. It can help you, over time, stop lying to yourself and improve your view of reality. The key is to use it effectively.

One key point, and one which will help you make decisions, is that any thought process that leads to your doing the irrational, is immoral – it is harmful to you. What is the connection between the decision and the action?

Essentially, the irrational is the wrong. It is based upon thoughts and ideas that contradict reality and because so it leads you into actions that are wrong or harmful. The irrational escapes being truthful because it is not arrived at by means of logic, clear definitions or realistic observations.

The irrational is anti-logic and anti-mind. It harms you because you do not see the damage it can do to you. You have either rationalized your conclusions based upon your emotions or you desire to have something that you do not deserve. The irrational always leads to a reversal of cause and effect and this means you are seeking the undeserved. The irrational also violates the code of morality that you establish for yourself by means of your best thought and desire for the good (your good). The irrational can also put others above you and send you on the path of trying to please them rather than follow your own logic. Whenever emotions come before reason, you are following the irrational.

Another aspect of this issue is the decision to take a chance or what is often called "a bold leap". It is certainly true that sometimes taking a chance works but it should not be that difficult to know what is right. This is because deciding what is right involves all your values as an integrated unit. If you find yourself in a position of doubt, ask yourself a basic question: "What do I love?" as it relates to this choice. This can often help set the correct context for a proper decision.

STEP 6. LEARN TO SEE REALITY

The key with this step is to know the difference between true knowledge (realism) and false knowledge (rationalizations). Once you acquire this ability, you can begin to base your actions on truth rather than falsehood.

I've written elsewhere that reason is "cognitive" in nature. When I say "cognitive", I mean that human thinking has the goal of understanding reality as it is. In other words, when you say "I see a table" you mean that you actually see the object that is defined as a "four-legged object with a flat surface". Apply this principle to your entire range of experience and you can understand that you can see reality as it is. This has important meaning for your quest to understand your addictions.

You might have been taught that the mind is incapable of judging and knowing reality but this view is part of the problem. How can a person "know" that drinking too much is bad; how can he know it with his mind if he has no confidence in his mind's ability to know? The first thing to recognize about commonly accepted pleasure choices is that many influences work against your understanding of how to make your own decisions. Advertising, television and movies provide a number of "arguments" for why it is good to engage in "out-of-context" pleasure pursuits. These arguments provide rationalizations for the pursuit of pleasure by attaching irresponsible behavior to "coolness" and "rebellion" – all of which lead impressionable people astray. It is up to you to straighten out the mess you have accepted into your life. You can only do this by questioning everything you have been taught and getting the issues straight in your mind.

At some point, you'll have to take a stand regarding the issue of what is real and what is not. You must then move from what is real to what is morally proper. The second should be based upon the first. Every is implies an ought. Without the "is", you will never arrive at the ought and you'll be perennially tied to the uncertainty which is the foundation of addiction.

To clarify for yourself what this means, make a list of the facts that you have identified that are important to your list of values and then define what you "ought" to do based upon those facts:

_____

_____

_____

_____

_____

_____

_____

_____

_____

_____

_____

_____

_____

_____

_____

_____

_____

_____

_____

_____

I learned that establishing knowledge today is very difficult because both religion and modern philosophy are bent on ensuring that you are confused about the nature of what is real. Yet, that knowledge is what you need in order to understand the world and how your problems fit in.

So what should you do? Challenge your family, your teachers, your professors and everyone you have known in your life? They all tell you they are certain there is no such thing as certainty. Yet, your mind *is* capable of understanding reality. There are certain truths that hold and it is possible for you to discover those truths. Existence exists and it is the job of your mind to understand it.[4]

If you were to take a walk around your local community and then identify some key things that you see and then answer the following questions:

- Is it real?

_____

_____

_____

_____

_____

_____

_____

_____

_____

_____

_____

_____

_____

_____

_____

_____

_____

_____

_____

_____

_____

_____

---

[4] I am not the first person to say this. Ayn Rand developed an entire philosophy of life around these propositions.

_____

- How do I know it?

_____
_____
_____
_____
_____
_____
_____
_____
_____
_____
_____
_____
_____
_____
_____
_____
_____
_____
_____
_____

- How can I discover it?

_____
_____
_____
_____
_____
_____

_____

_____

_____

_____

_____

_____

_____

_____

_____

_____

_____

_____

- How does it relate to all other real things in my surroundings?

_____

_____

_____

_____

_____

_____

_____

_____

_____

_____

_____

_____

_____

_____

_____

_____

_____

_____

- How does it relate to the actions I need to take to advance my life and happiness?

_____

_____

_____

_____

_____

_____

_____

_____

_____

_____

_____

_____

_____

_____

_____

_____

_____

_____

_____

_____

_____

_____

- What is the conclusion that you draw from this walk today?

_____
_____
_____
_____
_____
_____
_____
_____
_____
_____
_____
_____
_____
_____
_____
_____
_____
_____
_____

My philosophical role model said it best: "Existence exists—and the act of grasping that statement implies two corollary axioms: that something exists which one perceives and that one exists possessing consciousness, consciousness being the faculty of perceiving that which exists."[5]

Rather than wonder who you should please and for whom

---

[5] Ayn Rand, Galt's Speech, Atlas Shrugged

you should give up your happiness, your goal should be to develop a certainty about the nature of reality and using your knowledge to identify your values and how you will accomplish them.

More notes:

_____

_____

_____

_____

_____

_____

_____

_____

_____

_____

_____

_____

_____

_____

_____

_____

_____

_____

_____

_____

STEP 7. UNDERSTAND HOW VALUES CAN BE DISTORTED

Recall the work we did on your values. Step 7 builds upon this. It revolves around the idea that you are addicted to the excessive, out of context and harmful pursuit of pleasures that violates your values. You must understand how your values are being distorted by arguments that tell you it is "ok" to pursue those excessive pleasures. This is where you take ownership of your values and give yourself the true reasons why you should modulate and control your pleasures.

To get there, you must understand the true role of pleasure in life so you can analyze where you are going wrong.

Pleasure is something you need; pleasure is a value that signifies a moral life, or at the very least, that you are living in a condition in which pleasure is one of the rewards. Pleasure has an antipode which is pain. Both are built into the human body as signals through which the body communicates whether one is living well or not.

As we have pointed out, when we are young we sometimes become attracted to a particular form of pleasure and want to experience it as much as possible. Because of our inexperience, we are often not able to put pleasure in its proper context as a value and instead wrongly decide that the more pleasure (of a certain type) we experience, the better.

In those early days, the idea that pleasure is good was a foregone conclusion for you. You were simply too young and inexperienced to know better. Later, when you should know better, you see that pleasure conflicts with other values and sometimes other people. This is when you give your mind the order to find all the reasons why the pleasure is preferable to living a normal life. When experiencing that pleasure requires that you lie to yourself, your life gets distorted by the experience and the singular pleasure becomes your prime value over other high values. You descend into the depths of "low value" living.

Make a list of the arguments you use to lie to yourself and then write why they are wrong:

_____
_____
_____
_____
_____
_____
_____
_____
_____
_____
_____
_____
_____
_____
_____
_____
_____
_____
_____

The first thing to realize is that your value structure has been distorted by an over-emphasis on derivative pleasure values. We showed this clearly through the process of developing your values when we inserted certain pleasure choices into the list of values.

Pleasure, as such, is derived from mere sensations without intellectual content. Pleasure does not require values or intellectual content until the individual begins to conceptualize his values. The adult individual is then able to engage in reason which helps him establish a foundation of values without the need to pursue pleasure for its own sake. At this point, pleasure becomes integrated into the individual's value structure in a manner that advances life rather than destroys it.

Values are not apples on a tree that can be plucked and enjoyed; they are intellectual products of your mind. Real values are truly beneficial and go beyond immediate gratification. To live a better life, you must advance your thinking toward the intellectual and the real. Values are good for you in reality long-term – but it takes your mind and consistent action to make them real.

The key for you is to identify when you lie to yourself. This could include lying to justify drinking, using drugs, eating too much, watching too much television, having too much sex and any number of activities that result in a distorted value structure.

Next, you should consciously reject your subconscious value structure. If you feel the urge to engage in pleasurable activity, you must debate how excessive pleasure choices sabotage your value structure.

Then, you have to re-affirm the reasons for your value structure and see clearly the damage being done to it by an out-of-context focus on pleasure. This is a positive process that takes practice and conviction. It takes the certainty that a good value structure is the best and only way that one can accomplish certitude and happiness.

Next, you must repeat your argument daily until you understand that violating your value structure is as dangerous as death, that it is evil and that it could destroy your life. Convince yourself that going-outside-your-value context is distasteful, low and crass and you're starting to get it. You must consider the violation of your integrity to be a grave assault on your life and your happiness; so grave that to do it would be the epitome of stupidity and evil.

Let's make some notes now on how your addictive behavior destroys your value structure. Use these notes later to get these points clear in your mind:

_____
_____
_____
_____
_____
_____
_____
_____
_____
_____

_____

_____

_____

_____

_____

_____

_____

_____

_____

_____

Consider what this means. Smoking is dangerous, it smells bad, yellows your teeth and you could die from it. Your lungs get filled up with smoke and dangerous particles that block your air passages; you are susceptible to more colds and other diseases; you harm not only your lungs but your blood circulation and you could shorten your life. Get the picture?

How about drinking? You could get arrested and go to jail which would embarrass you with your family and friends. You could lose your job. You could kill someone in a bar fight (or drinking and driving) or you might do things so terrible that you would destroy your reputation and your present living standard. Drinking (and driving) could completely destroy your life; you could die or spend the rest of your life digging out from the mess you have made.

Make these arguments as starkly realistic as possible and see the true evil outcomes that could plague your life forever. You could die a failure while your children hate you for what you have done to them. Your wife will no longer respect you, not want to make love to you, even divorce you and throw you out on the street.

To overcome all the lies that you tell yourself takes discipline and thought. It takes clear thinking and logic in order to see the real benefits of your values and the real dangers of your subconscious adherence to false values. You should "know" your values and clearly see their impact on your life.

The difference between pursuing rational values and acting irrationally is an important distinction to keep in mind. For instance, let's look at sex. Sex is, for most people, something their body tells them feels good. In fact, it feels very good especially if you have sex with someone with whom you share values, experiences and ideas. Sex is fabulous. But finding an optimized sexual experience can be difficult. You must find a person for whom sex is a reward rather than just a thing to do.

If sex is just a thing to do, rather than a deeply enjoyable value accompanying other high values, then it tends to be promiscuous, meaningless, cynical and addictive. Thinking that sex for the sake of sex is a good thing is the first lie you tell yourself. The lie of casual sex can be very compelling but it leads to a dead end because it is limited in its meaning and pleasure.

I am not a psychologist so I don't know if it is possible, once one has gone through addiction, to ever have a "natural" value structure. The thought process and lies that led to addiction, cannot be easily displaced. This is why I think one has to completely eliminate the pleasure of addiction by avoiding the act all together at first. You might call it going cold turkey but certainly there has to be a period during which you regain control over your actions regarding the addiction.

Notes and Ideas:

_____

_____

_____

_____

_____

_____

_____

_____

_____

_____

_____

_____

_____

_____

_____

_____

_____

_____

_____

_____

STEP 8. KNOW WHAT ADDICTION IS

In my view, addiction is not merely physical; rather it is also mental and especially emotional. It has an intellectual component that is more powerful than the mere physical attraction of pleasure. *Addiction is an excuse for telling your mind to tell your body that it needs your pleasure choice and that you have no choice about that need; in fact, it argues, you should want that pleasure choice as a key value.* With addiction, your subconscious mind tells your conscious mind that your chosen pleasure is necessary. At the same time your mind is telling you that you are not addicted and that you have control of your life.

Why do I say it that way? Why do I say you are telling your mind to tell your body that it needs your pleasure of choice? I say it this way because I want to make it clear that you are engaged in a form of "sleight of hand" with your own mind. In a sense, it is a form of dishonesty through disintegration of your mind.

When you want to do something you should not do, you sense that you need a way to justify your choice. You experience the feeling of being wrong so you need to be able to tell yourself *subconsciously* that you should convince yourself that it is not really bad. This subconscious thought process is difficult to detect through introspection but if can develop the ability to identify this process and push yourself to avoid rationalizing bad behaviors, you can change and improve your moral stature.

By connecting your judgment to reality, you provide yourself with a powerful tool for understanding what drives you to your addictions. By observing what you are doing subconsciously, you will be able to gain control over those thought processes and see where you are going wrong. Then, when you next arrive at a decision point, you will be able to understand and control how you are deceiving yourself. With practice, you can gain control of those decision events and begin to make correct decisions based upon your values.

This book also provides you with valuable tips to helping you understand the process you use to justify harming yourself. Understanding how other people have dealt with addiction can help you see the process from the outside so you can compare the experiences of others to your own.

With this set of notes, identify, as clearly as possible, those steps you take of telling your mind to lie to you. It may take some work but once you identify and improve your ability to introspect, you'll start making tremendous progress with eliminating your addiction.

_____
_____
_____
_____
_____
_____
_____
_____
_____
_____
_____
_____
_____
_____
_____
_____
_____

STEP 9. STOP BAD RELATIONSHIPS

One of the best things you can do for yourself is to get certain people out of your life. These are people who engage in bad behavior with you, people who support your rationalizations and encourage you to engage in your addiction.

Face it, these people are not going to help you improve your life. They are only going to make it harder for you to decide about correct action because they are constantly sharing your addiction with you. Remember, these people are addicted too, and they, like you are often teetering on a precipice and often unable to resist the addiction which you have shared with them. You each represent the "tipping point" for each other and it is much better for you and him or her if you do not expose yourselves to that point – together.

It could be helpful for both of you that you explain to your friend that you have made the decision to avoid him or her because you want to eliminate, as much as possible the temptation you both share together. You may be surprised to find out that he is struggling in the same way. So, in some cases, the two of you might be able to agree that seeing each other is harmful.

On the other hand, there is absolutely no problem with just removing these people from your life, don't call them, don't meet them out, don't even engage in conversation with them. You will be much better off without them.

Notes:

_____

_____

_____

_____

_____

_____

_____

_____

_____

_____

_____

_____

_____

_____

_____

_____

_____

_____

_____

STEP 10. NOW START AGAIN

One thing I discovered after I had stopped drinking was that dealing with addiction was not over. In fact, I learned that I had more than one addiction and that eliminating one of them caused my addictive behavior to migrate to another form. You may find that after you have made significant progress in your addiction to alcohol, for example, you migrate to eating more food or having more sex or smoking more marijuana.

Addiction can migrate from one substance or activity to another. This is because it is a thought process that affects all of your thinking. It is a premise that influences all premises involving human action. As such, addition will can a place in any part of a man's value structure. Remember, the process is subconscious and any anti-value you have accepted will rise to the surface and take over when one anti-value is exposed and eliminated.

But now you have the tools you need to examine and explore this new area and correct your thinking. Again, remember that you have subconsciously chosen this next phase of your addiction. You now have the tools to help you understand what you are doing with your mind and you can defeat this addiction and the next if necessary. Once you have identified the next addiction, you need only start over with Step 1.

_____

_____

_____

_____

_____

_____

_____

_____

_____

_____

_____

_____

_____

_____

_____

_____

_____

_____

_____

_____

_____

_____

_____

_____

_____

_____

_____

_____

_____

_____

_____

_____

_____

_____

_____

_____

_____

_____

_____

_____

These ten steps can provide you with a foundation upon which to base your escape from addiction. It enables you to develop a strong value-base that becomes like a solid rock upon which you can base your life and find happiness. It is not an easy road but thinking and knowing are never easy.

THE TEN COMMANDMENTS OF DRINKING AND DRIVING

This section is intended as a reminder for readers who are presently working on their lives but have not yet stopped driving impaired.

I don't believe that morality should be based on commandments from a divine authority. However, some people respond better to direct commands – if only as reminders of what a proper morality would be.

So here are the Ten Commandments of Drinking and Driving. Remember, only criminals drink and drive.

I. If you are at home and you have had one or more drinks, STAY HOME.

_____
_____
_____
_____
_____
_____
_____
_____
_____
_____

II. If you are at a friend's house and you have had one or more drinks, STAY THERE, CALL A CAB OR HAVE SOMEONE DRIVE YOU HOME.

_____
_____
_____
_____
_____
_____
_____
_____
_____
_____
_____

III.   If you are planning an evening out with friends, DON'T GO OUT WITHOUT A DESIGNATED DRIVER.

_____
_____
_____
_____
_____
_____
_____
_____
_____

IV. If you are driving a group of people to a place where alcohol will be consumed, YOU ARE THE DESIGNATED DRIVER. Don't drink and drive.

_____
_____
_____
_____
_____

_____
_____
_____
_____
_____
_____

V. If you drive to a place where alcohol is being consumed,
YOU CANNOT DRINK or

_____
_____
_____
_____
_____
_____
_____
_____
_____

VI. If you drive to a place and have had one or more drinks,
CALL A CAB OR HAVE SOMEONE DRIVE YOU HOME.

_____
_____
_____
_____
_____
_____
_____

_____

_____

VII. If you drink and drive and think you will never get caught YOU WILL GET CAUGHT (and hope you do before you kill someone).

_____

_____

_____

_____

_____

_____

_____

_____

_____

_____

VIII. If you think that the police are jerks for pulling you over and charging you with a DUI, GO TO A COUNSELOR (because your actions are not the fault of the police--and you should go to a counselor anyway).

_____

_____

_____

_____

_____

_____

_____

_____

_____

_____

IX. If you think that taking a chance on driving while drunk is socially acceptable, YOU ARE A CRIMINAL and your social group is a bunch of criminals.

_____

_____

_____

_____

_____

_____

_____

_____

_____

X. If you think that you will never suffer from taking a chance on driving while drunk, YOU MIGHT AS WELL TELL YOUR FAMILY AND FRIENDS THAT YOU WANT TO LOSE YOUR JOB, YOUR DRIVERS LICENSE, KILL YOURSELF AND KILL SOMEONE ELSE (because sooner or later one or all of those things will happen)

_____

_____

_____

_____

_____

_____

_____

_____

_____

MYTHS OF DRINKING AND DRIVING:

Myth #1. I am too much of a man to let alcohol impair me. Besides only sissies can't handle drink.

Answer: People who do not drink are smarter than you.

_____
_____
_____
_____
_____
_____
_____
_____
_____
_____
_____

Myth #2. The police are just a bunch of jerks that want to stop people from having a good time.

Answer: You will have a "good time" after you have killed someone while drinking and driving.

_____
_____
_____
_____
_____
_____
_____
_____
_____
_____

Myth #3. I drink only to relax.

Answer: You drink to get high. You can't handle life straight.

_____

_____

_____

_____

_____

_____

_____

_____

_____

_____

Myth #4. After a long day's work, I deserve a good drink.

Answer: Why does your life require a foreign substance that changes your mental state? If you have worked hard, your body deserves rest not the abuse that alcohol gives it. Get a massage.

_____

_____

_____

_____

_____

_____

_____

_____

_____

_____

Myth #5. I'll never get caught drinking and driving.

Answer: You are a criminal who violates the law. Like any criminal, you deserve to be in jail because society is better off without you on the street.

_____
_____
_____
_____
_____
_____
_____
_____
_____
_____
_____

Myth #6. I can drive normally when I drink.

Answer: Not true. But that isn't important. You are still a criminal when you drink and drive.

_____
_____
_____
_____
_____
_____
_____
_____
_____
_____

Myth #7. I'm not a criminal if I drink and drive and don't get caught.

Answer: Not true. You are a criminal. Just like any criminal...you think you will never get caught...do you know any criminals who haven't spent time in jail? Do you know any criminals who admit they actually committed a crime? What does that make you?

_____

_____

_____

_____

_____

_____

_____

_____

_____

_____

_____

Myth #8. It's ok to have one or two drinks and drive.

Answer: It's not ok. You are still drinking and driving and could still get arrested—or worse, you could have an accident.

_____

_____

_____

_____

_____

_____

_____

_____

_____

_____

_____

Myth #9. If I drink and drive, I won't have an accident.

Answer: Sooner or later you will have an accident.

_____

_____

_____

_____

_____

_____

_____

_____

_____

_____

_____

Myth #10. Drinking and driving is no big deal. People do it all the time.

Answer: You say that to yourself because you just don't want to stop drinking and you're taking a chance on ruining the rest of your life.

_____

_____

_____

_____

_____

_____

_____

_____

_____

_____

_____

Myth #11. Drinking makes me feel more adult.

Answer: Feeling and being are two different things. Only adults are legally allowed to drink. Adults often act worse than children when they drink.

_____

_____

_____

_____

_____

_____

_____

_____

_____

_____

Note: Just think, if you didn't believe in these myths, you might actually be a respectable citizen. You might even be a non-drinker.

ONLY CRIMINALS DRINK AND DRIVE

Additional Space for Notes and Ideas:

_____

_____

_____

_____

_____

_____

_____

_____

_____

_____

_____

_____

_____

_____

_____
═══════════════════════════════

To order a copy of Mr. Villegas's book *Alcoholism and Addiction – A Secular Ten-Step Program*, go to:

http://amzn.to/2dOVXal